The Crisp Ap

WORDPERFECT

sorting made easy

by Patricia Fordham

Editor: David Foster
Project Manager: David Foster
Interior Design: Kathleen Gadway
Cover Design: Kathleen Gadway

Library of Congress No 93-70780

ISBN 1-56052-218-6

Dedicated to the Memory
of
Allien Russon
Business Educator

Mentor and Friend

Crisp Computer Book Series

These books are not like other books. Inspired by the widely successful "Fifty-Minute" Crisp Books, these books provide the least you need to know in order to use today's most popular application software packages. Specifically designed for either self-study or business training, they are "the fifty-minute books that teach!"

These guides are not for technical wizards or power users. They are for the average businessperson who is not familiar with computers nor comfortable with a particular software package—such as WordPerfect, Lotus 1-2-3, or Excel.

In most everyday computer applications, employees, managers, and students do not need to learn every feature and capability of their software. What most business users want is simply the amount of knowledge—delivered as quickly and painlessly as possible—to perform specific duties: write the letter, report or newsletter; create the budget or sales forecast; set up a mailing list; and other important business tasks. These books use everyday business examples to guide readers step-by-step through just those commands that they will use most.

Concise and practical, the Crisp fifty-minute computer books provide quick, easy ways to learn today's most popular computer software applications.

Other Books in the Crisp Computer Series

Beginning DOS for Nontechnical Business Users
Gordon Kimbell
ISBN: 1-56052-212-7

Beginning Lotus for Nontechnical Business Users
L. Louise Van Osdol
ISBN: 1-56052-213-5

Beginning WordPerfect 5.1 for Nontechnical Business Users
Mark Workman
ISBN: 1-56052-214-3

Beginning Excel for Nontechnical Business Users
William Amadio
ISBN: 1-56052-215-1

DOS for WordPerfect Users
Pamela Mills and Barbara Mathias
ISBN: 1-56052-216-X

WordPerfect Styles Made Easy
Geraldine Mosher
ISBN: 1-56052-217-8

Getting Creative with Newsletters in WordPerfect
Sandy Zook
ISBN: 1-56052-219-4

Contents

To the Reader

WordPerfect Sorting Made Easy teaches readers how to sort information, both alphabetically and numerically. As you will see, this ability comes in handy when organizing reports, tables, and similar material.

Sorting is a powerful feature that quickly organizes information into a more usable form; for example, you can sort a large client list by last name in order to locate a specific name faster. By learning how to sort in WordPerfect, you don't have to master another software program in order to take advantage of this feature. Also you can easily sort your existing WordPerfect files, instead of having to convert or retype them into another program.

This book is organized into five key lessons that cover topics such as learning basic keystrokes, sorting in tables, sorting by paragraph, building databases, and creating select statements. Lesson 6 contains additional exercises that both reinforce what you learned and give you more examples of how to use this knowledge.

Each key lesson is broken down into several sections:

- Introductory page—explains what will be covered in the lesson.
- Basic Steps—discuss step-by-step what you will be doing next. Note, however, that you are *not* supposed to work through these steps at this point. They are provided so that you can mentally go over the process *before* actually touching the keys. This visualization method should help you to better understand the final goal before you start typing any data. These steps are also useful as a review after you finish the exercises; they provide a quick overview of the lesson in case you need to refresh your memory later.
- Numbered Exercises—take you keystroke-by-keystroke through each new topic. Here, you type in the data provided and see the results on your computer screen.
- Summary—reviews the important skills learned in the lesson.

I hope *WordPerfect Sorting Made Easy* will serve you well as both a starting point and an ongoing reference tool for working with this powerful feature.

LESSON

1

The Sort Menu

Overview

The Sort function is a convenient WordPerfect tool that can save you enormous amounts of time in data management. Sort can be used to sort information on a line (even in a table), through paragraphs, and in secondary database Merge files.

To acquaint yourself with the Sort screen, take a few minutes to read through the following overview of the basic Sort menu. Once you understand how sorting works, you will be able to "quick reference" any Sort function by using this convenient reference book.

Basic Steps

The Sort feature allows you to sort information both alphabetically and numerically. Combined with the Select feature, Sort will enable you to pull out similar information and organize reports and tables.

The following steps are intended to acquaint you with the basics of the Sort process and give you a quick reference for sorting. Exercises, found later in other parts of this book, will guide you through specific sorting examples.

- Press *Sort* (**Ctrl-F9**)

  The Sort menu offers you the following choices:

  > **1** Merge, **2** Sort, **3** Convert old Merge Codes.

- Choose Sort (2)

  The following prompt will appear in the lower left corner of the screen:

  > Input file to sort: (Screen)

  You may either sort the file on your screen or retrieve another document by pressing *Retrieve* (**Shift-F10**) and typing the name of the file you want to sort.

- Press **Enter**

  The following prompt will appear in the lower left corner of the screen:

  Output file for sort: (Screen)

  You may choose to have the results of the sort come to the screen or create a new file on disk with a new file name.

  NOTE: To avoid information loss when sending sort information to a floppy disk, give the sort output a new file name. The sorted information will be sent automatically to the new file created on the disk.

- Press **Enter**

  The Sort screen will appear with the document in the top half of the screen window and the Sort menu in the bottom half of the screen window, as shown in Figure 1-1.

Figure 1-1

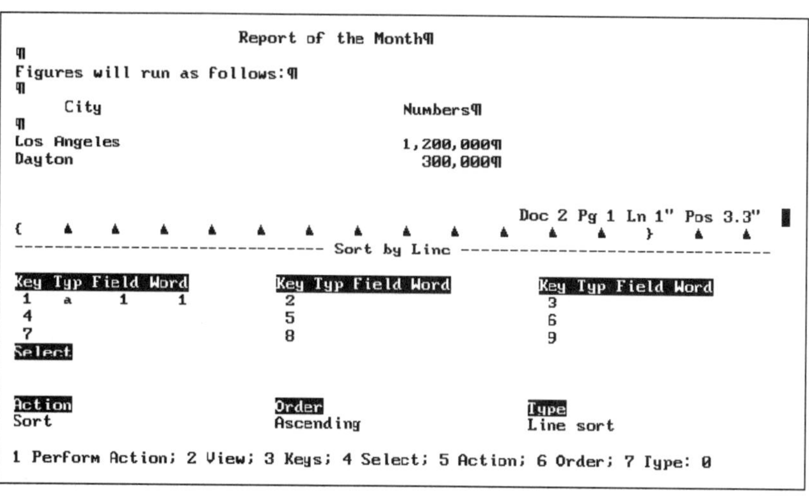
Report of the Month¶
¶
Figures will run as follows:¶
¶
City Numbers¶
¶
Los Angeles 1,200,000¶
Dayton 300,000¶

Doc 2 Pg 1 Ln 1" Pos 3.3"

Sort by Line

Key	Typ	Field	Word	Key	Typ	Field	Word	Key	Typ	Field	Word
1	a	1	1	2				3			
4				5				6			
7				8				9			

Select

Action: Sort
Order: Ascending
Type: Line sort

1 Perform Action; 2 View; 3 Keys; 4 Select; 5 Action; 6 Order; 7 Type: 0

There are other sorts to choose from: merge, paragraph, and table. You can change the type of sort by choosing **T**ype (7).

The parts of the Sort menu include the following:

Heading - type of sort (default is Sort by Line)

Key fields - where information is set for sorting priority in up to nine keys (1 through 9), depending on how you want the information sorted

Information area - displays current sort settings, including the order (ascending or descending), and the type of sort.

Sort menu - options for changing sort information and performing the sort

- Press **K**eys (3)

  The Key fields are designed for you to choose the criteria by which your information will be sorted.

  a - alphanumeric, which includes both letters and numbers of equal lengths

  n - numeric, which can be used when you have numbers of unequal lengths

  The Sort keys will remain the same during your computer session, giving you the advantage of sorting several files using the same key priorities.

- Press *Exit* (**F7**)

  You will return to the selection menu for sorting.

- Decide on the **O**rder (6) for the sort

  You can sort by ascending or descending order alphabetically or numerically. Once all the criteria are in place, you may perform the sort.

- Press **P**erform Action (1)

  While WordPerfect is sorting, a counter at the bottom of the screen tells you how many records are being sorted.

Lesson 1 Summary

The basic keystrokes for the Sort function are:

Press *Sort* (**CTRL F9**)

Choose Sort (2)

Press **Enter**

Press **Enter**

Choose Type (7)

Select the type of sort

Choose Keys (3)

Select the sorting criteria

Press *Exit* (**F7**)

Choose Order (6)

Select the sorting order

Choose Perform Action (1)

Notes

Notes

LESSON

2

Sorting by Line

Sorting by line is the most commonly used sorting function; WordPerfect's default setting is to sort by line. Each line separated by either a soft return [SRt] or a hard return [HRt] is considered a separate record. The Sort feature allows you to put these records into the order you desire.

In this lesson, you will learn the basics for sorting by line. As you work through the exercises, you will learn valuable techniques and hints that will increase your expertise in sorting by line.

Basic Steps

Sorting by line is the most commonly used type of sort. When you have information to sort alphabetically, such as last names, or you want to sort by state in an address database, sorting by line is the type of sort to use. The basic steps for sorting by line are as follows:

- Press *Sort* (**Ctrl-F9**)

  Three sort options appear:

  1 Merge **2** Sort **3** Convert Old Merge Codes

- Select Sort

  The prompt in the lower left corner of the screen tells you

  Input file to sort: (Screen)

  This is the location of the unsorted information. You can either bring a file into the screen before you press *Sort* or bring a file in at this point. To bring a file in from the disk, type the directory and name of the file (for example—SORT1).

- Press **Enter**

  The prompt in the lower left corner of the screen indicates

  Output file for sort: (Screen)

  You may choose to have the results of the sort come to the screen or go to a new file on disk with a new file name.

  NOTE: To avoid information loss in an existing file, give the output file a new name. The sorted information will be sent automatically to the new file created on the disk.

- Press **Enter**

  The type of sort defaults to Sort by Line. Check to make sure that the heading of the Sort menu indicates Sort by Line.

- Press **K**eys (3)

  There are four Key priority headings:

Key	Typ	Field	Word
1	a	1	1

  Key1 is your first priority for the sort. Typ (meaning "type") specifies either an alphanumeric sort (can include both numbers and alphabetical characters) or a numeric sort (used for uneven sets of numbers or numbers only). Field and Word allow you to select record subdivisions, depending on the type of records you are sorting.

  You can use up to nine keys for sort criteria. For example, one key is sufficient if you want to sort lines by the first word in the line. Use additional keys if you want to sort lines by the second word for lines that begin with the same word. Alternatively, you can set up one sort key to sort lines by words other than the first word in each line. To do this, enter another number for the position of the word on which you want to sort. For example, enter 2 for sort key1's Word setting to sort lines by the second word in each line. Another way to do this is to use a minus sign (-) for the sort key's Word setting. For example, the setting -1 causes WordPerfect to sort lines by the first word at the end of each line.

- Press *Exit* (**F7**)

  You will return to the Sort menu options.

- Choose **O**rder (6) (optional)

  You may choose to sort in ascending (A to Z) or descending (Z to A) order.

- Select **V**iew (2) (optional)

  The View option lets you scroll through the information in your document without exiting the Sort screen. To return to the Sort menu, press *Exit* (**F7**).

- Select **P**erform Action (1)

  The sort will begin.

Sorting by Line

When you sort by line, each line is considered a separate record where the information on each line is kept together. The following exercises will help you understand how sorting by line can help you organize your information.

Exercise 2.1 Sorting by First Name

1. Type in the following list of names at the left margin. Be sure to put one hard return **[HRt]** at the end of each name and only one space between each individual part of the name.

   Dana L. Bell
   Cindy Herron
   Sherri Simons
   Diane Birk
   Nicki Chidester
   Jonathan O. Jones
   Jeffery D. Simons

2. Press *Save* (**F10**) and name the file **SORT1** (specify a drive and directory if necessary)

   This will "safety" save the list.

   You are now ready to sort the list alphabetically. Your cursor may be anywhere in your document.

3. Press *Sort* (**Ctrl-F9**)
4. Choose Sort (2)
5. Press **Enter** twice (accepting the file on screen for input and directing the output to the screen)

   Your menu should look like the one in the Figure 2-1.

Figure 2-1

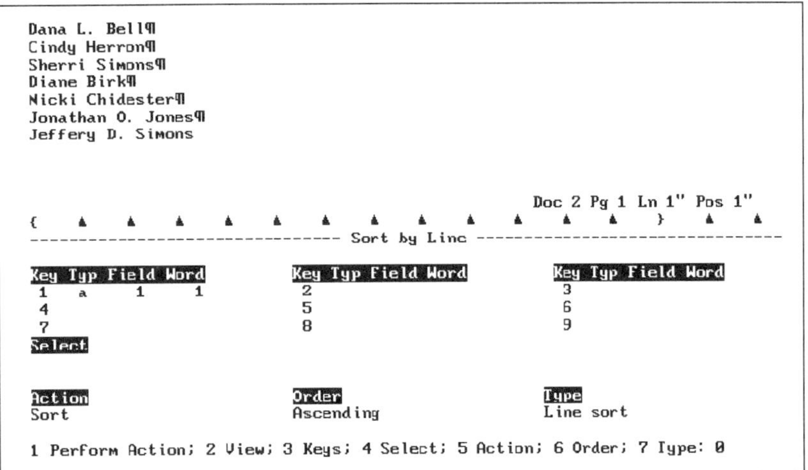

The Sort screen has defaulted to Sort by Line. Look at the key1 example. You will sort alphabetically, by first name, which is the first word in the first field. Accept the default setting as shown.

6. Select Perform Action (1)

   The result should appear as follows:

   Cindy Herron
   Dana L. Bell
   Diane Birk
   Jeffery D. Simons
   Jonathan O. Jones
   Nicki Chidester
   Sherri Simons

7. Press *Save* (**F10**)

   Save the file as **SORT2** (specify a path if necessary). Your document will still be on the screen.

Exercise 2.2 Sorting by Last Name

Use the list you created in Exercise 2.1.

1. Press *Sort* (**Ctrl-F9**)
2. Select Sort (2)
3. Press **Enter** twice

   This directs the sort output to the screen and brings up the Sort menu.

   Notice that two last names in the file are spelled the same (Simons). You will need to add a second sort key for the first names because of the identical last names.
4. Select **K**eys (3)

   Set up sort keys 1 and 2 as shown in Figure 2-2.

Figure 2-2

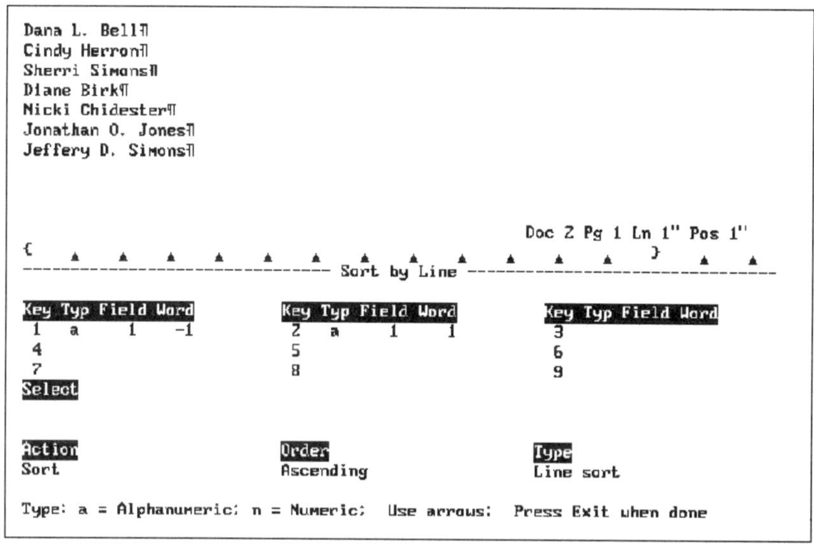

Some of the names have middle initials and some do not. Therefore, the -1 Word setting for sort key1 causes WordPerfect to sort by the first word at the right of each line (record). Without the minus sign, the sort priority would be the first word in each line.

5. Press *Exit* (**F7**)

   You will return to the Sort menu.

6. Select **P**erform Action (1)

   The names should appear in the following order:

   Dana L. Bell
   Diane Birk
   Nicki Chidester
   Cindy Herron
   Jonathan O. Jones
   Jeffery D. Simons
   Sherri Simons

7. Press *Exit* (**F7**) and select **N**o twice to clear the document window

You have seen how you can use a file on the screen to sort information. The next exercise will show you how to create a new file to store sorted information.

Exercise 2.3 New File Sort

1. Type the following list of names at the left margin:

   Dana
   Cindy
   Sherri
   Diane
   Nicki
   Jonathan
   Jeffery

2. *Save* (**F10**) the list with the filename **LIST**
3. Press *Sort* (**Ctrl-F9**) and choose Sort (2)
4. Press **Enter**

   Pressing **Enter** selects input from the screen.

5. For sort output, name your file **TEST1**
6. Press **Enter**

   The Sort menu appears.

7. Choose **K**eys (3)
8. Set the first sort key as follows:

Key	Typ	Field	Word
1	a	1	1

9. Press *Exit* (**F7**) to return to the Sort menu
10. Press Perform Action (1) to perform the sort

11. The sorted list should appear as follows in the TEST1 file:

    Cindy
    Dana
    Diane
    Jeffery
    Jonathan
    Nicki
    Sherri

Now you will look in the TEST1 file to see that the above list is there.

1. Press *List Files* (**F5**)

   If necessary, enter the correct path for the location of the TEST1 file.

2. Select the document named **LIST**

3. Choose Look (6) to view the contents of the file

   The list in this file is not alphabetized.

4. Press **Enter**

   You will return to List Files.

5. Select the document named **TEST1**

6. Choose Look (6) to see the list in the document named TEST1

   The list sent to the new file is alphabetized.

7. Press *Exit* (**F7**) twice to return to the document

Now let's take a further look at the field settings in the key priority area. The next section will give you an overview of sorting tabular columns and learning how to differentiate fields.

Sorting Tabular Columns

When using the Sort menu with tabular columns, you need to indicate which field to sort in. For the next exercise, use the document you have already created called SORT1.

Exercise 2.4 Sorting Tabular Columns

If necessary, press *Exit* (**F7**) and select No twice to clear the document window.

1. Press *Retrieve* (**Shift-F10**) to retrieve the file **SORT1** to the screen
2. Press *Reveal Codes* (**Alt-F3** or **F11**) to see the codes in the document
3. Press **Home, Home, Home, Up Arrow** to take you to the very beginning of the document
4. Press *Format* (**Shift-F8**)
5. Choose Line (1)
6. Select Tab Set (8)

   The tab ruler shows you the default tab settings at every five characters. By default, tabs are set "Relative to Margin."

   NOTE The WordPerfect tab default, Relative to Margin, means that the tab spacing is measured from the left margin. The other option for tabs is Absolute from the paper edge, which means the tab spacing is measured from the left edge of the paper. When you choose Relative to Margin, if you have to move the margins the tabs will automatically move with them and you will not have to reset your tabs—very convenient!

7. Press **Ctrl-End** to delete the existing tab settings

8. Press **3, Enter,** and **4, Enter,** to insert new tabs at 3 and 4 inches
9. Press *Exit* (**F7**) twice to return to the document screen
10. Position the cursor under the middle initial **L** in the name Dana L. Bell and press **Tab**

    This moves the L to the 4 inch position on the status line.
11. Position your cursor under the **B** in Bell and press **Tab** to move the name Bell to the 5 inch position on the status line
12. Tab all middle initials and last names as you did in the previous step. Where there is no middle initial, press **Tab** twice
13. Safety *Save* (**F10**) the new document by naming it **SORT3**

Because there are two last names that are spelled in the same way, you need to set the sort priority for a second key. This will tell WordPerfect to sort by first names for any records with the same last name.

1. Press *Sort* (**Ctrl-F9**)
2. Choose Sort (2)
3. Press **Enter** twice to accept the document on screen as the sort input and output locations
4. Press Keys (3) and clear the key settings by pressing **Ctrl-End**
5. Enter the information for keys 1 and 2 as follows:

Key	Typ	Field	Word	Key	Typ	Field	Word
1	a	3	-1	2	a	1	1

    With the document in tabular columns, the last name is in the third field. Because not all the names in the list have a middle initial, the last name will be sorted from the right with a -1 for Word. The negative number tells Sort to come from the right margin rather than the left margin.

6. Press *Exit* (**F7**) to return to the Sort menu
7. Press Perform Action (1) to perform the sort

   The result should look like this:

Dana	L.	Bell
Diane		Birk
Nicki		Chidester
Cindy		Herron
Jonathan	O.	Jones
Jeffery	D.	Simons
Sherri		Simons

8. Press *Reveal Codes* (**Alt-F3**) to turn off the code display

Sorting Within Tables

The Sort feature will work in a table environment; however, you must take into account some different parameters. When you do a table sort, you consider each row in the table as a record. The cells in the table are considered fields.

NOTE

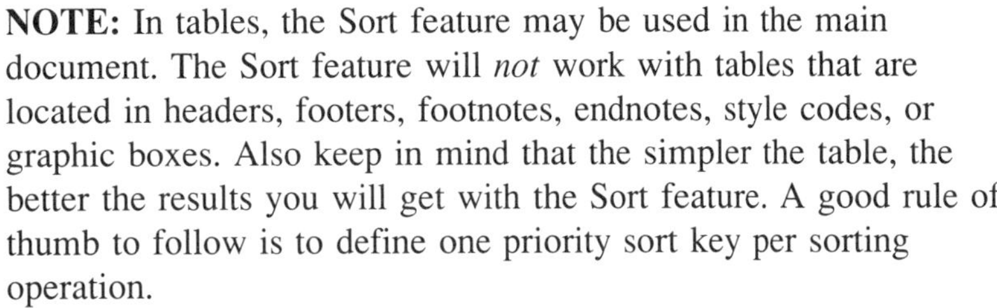

NOTE: In tables, the Sort feature may be used in the main document. The Sort feature will *not* work with tables that are located in headers, footers, footnotes, endnotes, style codes, or graphic boxes. Also keep in mind that the simpler the table, the better the results you will get with the Sort feature. A good rule of thumb to follow is to define one priority sort key per sorting operation.

Take time to work through the following exercise, which will show you the changes in the Sort menu terminology for tables and help you to understand how to indicate correct cell numbers for an accurate sort.

Exercise 2.5 Sorting Within Tables

Information that has been entered in a document may be placed in table format and then sorted.

1. Press *Exit* (**F7**) and then select No twice to clear the document window
2. Press *Retrieve* (**Shift-F10**) and retrieve the file **SORT1** that you created earlier

Now do the following steps to turn this list into a table.

1. Press *Format* (**Shift-F8**), choose Line (1), then Margins (7) to set the margins to 2 inches on each side

   The table you are going to create will configure to the margins.
2. Press *Exit* (**F7**) to return to the document
3. Press *Block* (**Alt-F4** or **F12**) (your cursor should be at the beginning of the document)

4. Press **Home, Home, Down Arrow** to block the entire list
5. Press *Columns/Table* (**Alt-F7**)
6. Select Table (2)
7. Choose Create (1)
8. Choose Tabular Column (1)

NOTE: The type of table you select (tabular or parallel column) will depend on the way you have set up the text. A tabular column is one in which the tab settings are used to define the columns in the table. The hard returns in the document will define the rows in the table. For parallel columns, the parallel column definitions are used to define the columns in the table, while the *Hard Page* [HPg] codes define the table rows.

Figure 2-3 shows our table. The names in the table are not in alphabetical order at this point. Notice that there is a menu of table edit options at the bottom of the screen. WordPerfect is now in Table Edit mode.

Figure 2-3

```
Dana L. Bell¶
Cindy Herron¶
Sherri Simons¶
Diane Birk¶
Nicki Chidester¶
Jonathan O. Jones¶
Jeffery D. Simons¶

Table Edit:  Press Exit when done        Cell A1 Doc 1 Pg 1 Ln 1.14" Pos 2.12"
Ctrl-Arrows Column Widths; Ins Insert; Del Delete; Move Move/Copy;
1 Size; 2 Format; 3 Lines; 4 Header; 5 Math; 6 Options; 7 Join; 8 Split: 0
```

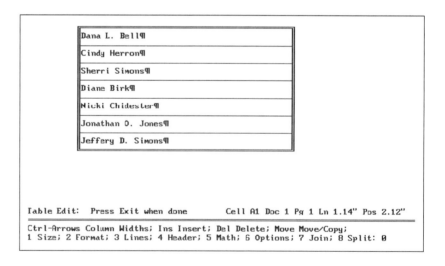

9. Press *Exit* (**F7**) to exit the Table Edit mode

In order to sort the names in the table by alphabetical order, use the following steps:

1. Press *Sort* (**Ctrl-F9**) and select Sort (2)

   The Sort screen appears immediately, bypassing the input file and output file prompts you see for other sorts. The heading on the Sort screen reads “Sort Table.”

2. Press **Ctrl-End** to clear the current sort key settings

3. Press **Keys** (3) and set sort key1 as follows:

Key	Typ	Cell	Line	Word
1	a	1	1	-1

   NOTE The priority settings for table sort keys have an extra category—Cell. The Cell setting specifies a specific cell number within table rows that contains the information on which you want to sort. The Line setting specifies lines within cells as subdivisions on which you can sort information. The Word setting sets the same priority for cell information as it does for sorting lines and paragraphs. You may use a positive or negative value for the Word setting to control which side of the lines the chosen word is to be considered for the sort.

4. Press *Exit* (**F7**) to return to the Sort menu

5. Select Perform Action (1) to sort the table by last name in alphabetical order

The sort should appears as follows:

Dana L. Bell
Diane Birk
Nicki Chidester
Cindy Herron
Jonathan O. Jones
Jeffery D. Simons
Sherri Simons

In order to protect information in its "purest" form, be sure to save your information *before* performing any sort procedure.

If you have a record containing a special designation, such as Jr., avoid sorting by the J in Jr. by putting a hard space (**Home-Spacebar**) between the last name and Jr. As the following example shows, when the sort is performed, the B in Bell will be the sort word, not Jr.

Dana L. Bell, Jr.   Dana L. Bell,[**Hard Space**]Jr.

Lesson 2 Summary

Sorting by Line

The Sort feature's default menu and most frequently used function is Sort by Line, where each line is considered a record and is separated by either a soft or a hard return. Sort by Line has a default priority key which can be changed to sort by any of the fields, lines, or words in the record. The sort may be performed with one priority key or with up to nine priority keys. You can use a negative value for the key's Word setting to sort on a word counted from the right side of the line. For example, in sorting by last name, where the name might contain a middle name or initial, coming from the right side will ensure a correct sort.

Sorting Tabular Columns

Tabs may be changed to accommodate sorting after a document has been created. Once the tabs have been set, the Sort menu can be activated and the priority keys identified as to which fields the sort is to take place in.

Sorting in Tables

Information that has been entered in a file may be placed in table format and then sorted. The area to be sorted is blocked and then the table is created, using the Tabular Column function. When *Sort* (**Ctrl-F9**) is selected, WordPerfect knows you are in a table format and the Table Sort menu appears automatically for keys to be defined and the sort to be performed.

Notes

Notes

Notes

LESSON

3

Sorting by Paragraph

The paragraph sort is the most flexible of the Sort menus because information can be entered in any way you desire—for example, as unstructured notes. All you have to do to indicate the end of a paragraph is enter two hard returns [HRt].

The flexibility of this type of database gives you tremendous leeway for organizing your data. However, this same flexibility also restricts the ways in which you can manipulate the information.

The next few pages will take you through the basics of sorting in the paragraph environment.

Basic Steps

The basic steps for sorting by paragraph are as follows:

- Press *Sort* (**Ctrl-F9**)
- Select Sort (2)

  A prompt will appear in the lower left corner of the screen:

  Input file to sort: (Screen)

  You are asked if you want to sort the file on your screen or bring a file in at this point by pressing *Retrieve* (**Shift-F10**) and naming the file you want to sort.
- Press **Enter**

  The following prompt will appear in the lower left corner of the screen:

  Output file for sort: (Screen)

  You may choose to have the results of the sort come to the screen or to create a new file on disk with a new file name.
- Press *Enter*

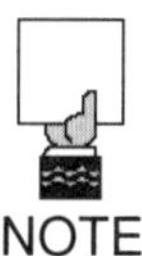

NOTE

  NOTE: If you choose to have the information go to the disk, you will want to avoid information loss in an existing file. Thus, you will want to give the output from the sort a new file name. The sorted information will then be sent automatically to the new file created on the disk.
- Select **T**ype (7) (optional)
- Choose **P**aragraph (3) (optional)
- Select **K**eys (3)

  There are four sort key settings for sorting by paragraph in each of the nine priority keys, as follows:

Key	Typ	Line	Field	Word
1	a	1	1	1

  After you have made your priority key assignments, return to the sort menu by pressing *Exit* (**F7**).
- Choose **P**erform Action (1) to initiate the sort

Paragraph Sorts

The paragraph may be considered one field or several fields. The amount of information in a field may be a character, several lines, or several pages. Each field can contain one line or several lines. The indication of [SRt] or [HRt] marks the end of a line. Two [HRt] mark the end of a paragraph record.

You can add some organization to the paragraph by establishing the same format for the first few lines of each record. Figure 3-1 illustrates how keeping the first line of organization the same in each record enables the Sort function to have common selectors. There are three records in the example—Dr. Timothy Hartman, Joshua Jensen, and Cindy Herron. The first line of each record gives the person's name, street address, city, state, and zip code. The rest of the individual record, however, contains information that is not organized into particular fields or lines where the data would be the same in each record. In this example, information can be sorted by the first line because the information is organized into fields within the records.

NOTE

NOTE: There will be times when you will want to sort only a portion of a document. The WordPerfect Block function enables you to block the information. By selecting the sort keys, priorities for sorting can be identified in the key area and the sort performed.

Figure 3-1

BOARD OF DIRECTORS

DIRECTOR	ADDRESS	CITY	STATE	ZIP
Dr. Timothy Hartman	1503 Hudson	Dallas	TX	54321

Occupation: Veterinarian for 12 years Hobbies: golf, swimming. Enjoys outdoor activities. Good contacts with community leaders. Married; three children ranging in age from 1 year to 15 years. Wife's profession: lawyer.

Joshua Jensen	Route 5	Morgan	UT	84305

Occupation: Rancher. Background: Bachelor's degree in Economics; teacher in public school system for five years. Married; five children (all are on their own, the youngest being 22). Brings strength to the Board by local community contacts. Wife is retired.

Cindy Herron	1432 Charlotte	Fairfax	VA	21302

Occupation: High School Counselor for three years. Background: teacher for five years in private education. Hobbies: poetry, radio commentator. Excellent communication skills. Married; two children ages five to twelve. Interested in racial and gender equality.

Exercise 3.1 Sorting Records by Paragraph

In this exercise, you will type in the Board of Directors information using these format settings:

1. Accept the default margins of 1 inch
2. Change the tab setting as follows:

   Press *Format* (**Shift-F8**), select Line (1), then choose Tabs (8), and clear the tabs by pressing **Ctrl-End**

   Now accept the default, Relative to the Margin, tab setting and set the tabs at 2, 4, 5, and 6 inches
3. Return to the document window by pressing *Exit* (**F7**)

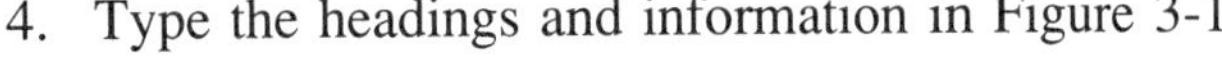

4. Type the headings and information in Figure 3-1
5. Position the cursor at the beginning of the first record (Dr. Timothy Hartman) and *Block* (**Alt-F4** or **F12**) all three records (through Cindy Herron)
6. Press *Sort* (**Ctrl-F9**)

   NOTE: With block on, the Sort screen appears immediately, thus eliminating input and output choices.
7. Select Type (7)
8. Select Paragraph (3) for type of sort
9. Select Keys (3) and define the priority settings:

   Last name:

Key	Typ	Line	Field	Word
1	a	1	1	-1

   City:

Key	Typ	Line	Field	Word
2	a	1	3	1

10. Press *Exit* (**F7**) to exit from the key definitions to the Sort menu
11. Select Perform Action (1) to complete the sort

    The completed sort will look like Figure 3-2.

Figure 3-2

BOARD OF DIRECTORS

DIRECTOR	ADDRESS	CITY	STATE	ZIP
Dr. Timothy Hartman	1503 Hudson	Dallas	TX	54321

Occupation: Veterinarian for 12 years Hobbies: golf, swimming. Enjoys outdoor activities. Good contacts with community leaders. Married; three children ranging in age from 1 year to 15 years. Wife's profession: lawyer.

Cindy Herron	1432 Charlotte	Fairfax	VA	21302

Occupation: High School Counselor for three years. Background: teacher for five years in private education. Hobbies: poetry, radio commentator. Excellent communication skills. Married; two children ages five to twelve. Interested in racial and gender equality.

Joshua Jensen	Route 5	Morgan	UT	84305

Occupation: Rancher. Background: Bachelor degree, in Economics; teacher in public school system for five years. Married; five children (all are on their own, the youngest being 22). Brings strength to the Board by local community contacts. Wife is retired.

12. Press *Save As* (**F10**) and save the file as **PARASORT**
13. Press *Exit* (**F7**) and select No twice to clear the document window

Special Paragraph Sorts

Bibliography

If you are using a bibliography format, WordPerfect considers the margin release as only one field because there are no tabs following that will define fields. To avoid a mix-up, use a -1 for the Field key settings. This tells WordPerfect to use the field *before* the first field as the sorting feature.

Exercise 3.2 Bibliography

1. Type the following text using bibliography format (*Indent* (**F4**), *Margin Release* (**Shift-Tab**))

   Wright, Simon. *I Will Go and Preach.* New York Publications, New York, 1993.

   Hanson, Wade. *To Each His Own.* Time Publications, Philadelphia, Family Enterprises, August, 1991.

   Birk, Kay. *The Middle Years.* Apex Publishers, New York, New York, Eastern Division, 1992.

2. *Block* (**Alt-F4** or **F12**) the bibliography records
3. Press *Sort* (**Ctrl-F9**)

   The Sort screen appears immediately.

4. Select Keys (3)
5. Press **Ctrl-End** to clear the current sort key settings
6. Set the first sort key as follows:

Key	Typ	Line	Field	Word
1	a	1	-1	1

7. Press *Exit* (**F7**) to return to the Sort menu

8. Press <u>P</u>erform Action (1)
9. Press *Save As* (**F10**) and save the file as **BIBSORT**
10. Press *Exit* (F7) and select <u>N</u>o twice to clear the document window

The bibliography information is sorted alphabetically by author in ascending order. Your bibliography should look like Fig 3-4.

Figure 3-3

Birk, Kay. *The Middle Years.* Apex Publishers, New York, New York, Eastern Division, 1992.

Hanson, Wade. *To Each His Own.* Time Publications, Philadelphia, Family Enterprises, August, 1991.

Wright, Simon. *I Will Go and Preach.* New York Publications, New York,
1993.

Tabular Columns

When you are creating a document that requires tabular columns and there are two hard returns between each record, use paragraph sort.

Exercise 3.3 Tabular Columns

1. Use *Format* (**Shift-F8**), Line (1), Margins (7) to set the left and right margins to 2 inches
2. Use *Format* (**Shift-F8**), Line (1), Tabs (8) to set tab stops at 1.75 and 3.5 inches
3. Type the following information with two hard returns ([HRt]) after each line, as follows:

CAT SHOW ASSIGNMENTS

Tammy	**Tabby**	**Long Hair**
David	**Parti-Color**	**Long Hair**
Kyle	**Smoke**	**Short Hair**
Ashley	**Black**	**Long Hair**

4. *Block* (**Alt-F4** or **F12**) the records
5. Press *Sort* (**Ctrl-F9**)
6. Clear the sort priority keys, if necessary (Keys (3), **Ctrl-End**)

7. To sort alphabetically by cat-owner names, press **K**eys (3) and set sort key1 as follows:

Key	Typ	Line	Field	Word
1	a	1	1	1

8. Press *Exit* (**F7**) to return to the Sort menu
9. Select **P**erform Action (1)

   The results should look like this:

CAT SHOW ASSIGNMENTS

Ashley	Black	Long Hair
David	Parti-Color	Long Hair
Kyle	Smoke	Short Hair
Tammy	Tabby	Long Hair

10. Press *Exit* (**F7**) and select **N**o twice to clear the document window

Lesson 3 Summary

Basic Steps

The basic steps used to get to the Sort menu are the same for both line sorts and paragraph sorts. At the Sort screen, however, the type of sort should be changed to "Sort by Paragraph."

The difference between paragraph sorts and line sorts is that there are two [HRt] between records in the paragraph sort rather than one.

In order to give WordPerfect uniform information with which to sort paragraphs, at least one line of information in each record needs to be consistent in terms of location of the fields and words.

Special Paragraph Sorts

Paragraph sorts may be used with a bibliography format or a tabular column setup.

Notes

Notes

Notes

LESSON

4

Sorting Merge Documents

Secondary files for merge operations must often be sorted. Within a secondary file are merge codes that enable the system to match the codes with identical codes in a primary merge file. One of the most common uses of WordPerfect's Merge feature is to store names and addresses in a database and merge them with a boilerplate (same information goes to all) file. Think of the hours a merge can save in such a situation.

Because information needs to be organized in a logical fashion to be useful, the Sort feature in WordPerfect can be a tool for you to sort your secondary database files before or after a merge of the database and boilerplate documents.

In the following section, you will build a short secondary merge database file and sort its records.

To help you to understand how Sort works with Merge database files, it is suggested that you go through the exercise in this lesson. Because working with computer software is a perceptual-motor skill (a skill that involves observing *and* doing), the time you give to perceiving the idea and going through the motions can give you an understanding of the powerful possibilities of the combination of Merge and Sort.

Basic Steps

WordPerfect 5.1 lets you establish field names before you create a secondary document. This gives you a format to follow for all your records. The basic steps for creating a secondary merge database are as follows.

- Press **Shift-F9**
- Choose More (6)
- Highlight {FIELD NAMES}
- Press **Enter**
- Enter your field names
- Press *Exit* (**F7**) to stop adding fields to your database and begin adding data

The Secondary Merge File

It is a good idea to store all your records in a secondary merge file where you can add and delete information as you desire. Your database may contain as many records as you want or as your computer's memory will allow.

Once you have created your secondary merge file, you can use WordPerfect's *Window* (**Ctrl-F3**) feature to place the database document in the top window and create the boilerplate in the bottom window of the split screen. Thus, you will be able to see what is in your database file while creating your boilerplate (or primary) file. You no longer have to write down what you named or numbered a field—the file will be before your eyes as you need the information.

About the Secondary File Structure

WordPerfect uses two codes to indicate the structure of your database:

- {END FIELD} **F9** represents the end of information you want in a field. You can, however, include more than one line in a field.
- {END RECORD} **Shift-F9** represents the end of information for a given record. When you enter the {END RECORD} code, WordPerfect inserts a page break (double-dashed line), which it uses to determine where the record ends.

Exercise 4.1 Building and Sorting a Secondary Merge File

1. Press *Merge* (**Shift-F9**)
2. Choose <u>M</u>ore (6)

   The cursor will move to the Merge command programming window where additional merge codes are located.
3. Type <u>F</u>

   The highlight moves to the {FIELD}Field~ code.
4. Move the highlight to the {FIELD NAMES} code
5. Press **Enter**

   A prompt for the first field (Field 1) appears in the lower- left corner of the screen.
6. Type **NAME** and press **Enter**

   The prompt for the second field appears.
7. Type **COMPANY** and press **Enter**

   The prompt for the third field appears.

8. Type **ADDRESS** and press **Enter**

   There will be only three fields in this exercise. So when the prompt for Field 4 appears,

9. Press *Exit* (**F7**)

   The field merge codes for your secondary file will appear at the top of the screen. In the bottom left corner will be instructions to enter Field:NAME.

Now you are ready to enter the data in your secondary merge file.

1. Enter the name **Colonel Dan Simmons** (do *not* press **Enter**)
2. Press **F9**

   An {END FIELD} code marks the end of the field. At the bottom of the screen in the left corner will be instructions to enter Field:COMPANY.

3. Type **USMC** and press **F9**

   A prompt for the ADDRESS field appears.

4. Type **Camp Hollister** and press **Enter**
5. Type **North Carolina 23489** and press **F9**

NOTE

   NOTE: Type the entire address before adding an {END FIELD} code at the end of the address. You will enter the first line of the address without an {END FIELD} code. This will keep all of the address in one field.

6. Press **Shift-F9** and select End Record (2)

   An {END RECORD} code and a hard return are inserted.You will also see a double dashed line. You are now ready for the next record. The field indication in the left corner at the bottom of the screen says Field:NAME.

7. Enter the following data for the next two records by repeating steps 1 through 6

   Mr. Dana L. Peterson{END FIELD}
   Computer Specialists{END FIELD}
   #7 Highland Hills
   Albany, New York 20021{END FIELD}
   {END RECORD}

   Mrs. Diane Birk{END FIELD}
   Executive Development{END FIELD}
   1509 Avenue of the Americas Suite 2
   New York, New York 10021{END FIELD}
   {END RECORD}

8. Safety *Save* (**F10**) the document by naming it **DATABASE**

Now let's sort the records in your database.

1. Press *Sort* (**Ctrl-F9**) and choose Sort (2)
2. Press **Enter** twice to have the sort saved to the screen
3. Select Type (7) and choose Merge (1)
4. Press Keys (3) and set the first sort key as follows:

Key	Typ	Line	Field	Word
1	a	1	1	-1

   These settings will cause the sort to be done on the last names in the records.
5. Press *Exit* (**F7**) to return to the Sort menu
6. Perform the sort now by choosing Perform Action (1)
7. Press *Save As* (**F10**) and save the file as **DATASORT**

   The resulting sort should appear as shown in Figure 4-1.

Figure 4-1

```
{FIELD NAMES}NAME~COMPANY~ADDRESS~~{END RECORD}¶
================================================================================
Mrs. Diane Birk{END FIELD}¶
Executive Development{END FIELD}¶
1509 Avenue of the Americas Suite2¶
New York, New York 10021{END FIELD}¶
{END RECORD}¶
================================================================================
Mr. Dana L. Peterson{END FIELD}¶
Computer Specialists{END FIELD}¶
#7 Highland Hills¶
Albany, New York 20021{END FIELD}¶
{END RECORD}¶
================================================================================
Colonel Dan Simmons{END FIELD}¶
USMC{END FIELD}¶
Camp Hollister¶
North Carolina 23489{END FIELD}¶
{END RECORD}¶
================================================================================

C:\WPDOCS\DATASORT                                      Doc 1 Pg 1 Ln 1" POS 1"
```

8. Press *Exit* (**F7**) and select No twice to clear the document window

Once the database is sorted according to your needs, you can merge the database with your primary documents (consult the *Merge* section of *WordPerfect* documentation for instructions on how to prepare a primary document to merge with a database). Your database may be sorted with different priority keys for various results.

Using the Block Command

You can also sort a secondary file using the Block command. Here are the basic steps for this operation:

- Press *Block* (**Alt-F4** or **F12**)
- Press *Sort* (**Ctrl-F9**)

  You will go directly to the Sort Secondary Merge File screen.
- Select Keys (3) and prioritize your information in the key area
- Press *Exit* (**F7**) to return to the Sort menu
- Press Perform Action (1)

Exercise 4.2 Block Sort

1. Type the following list of names at the left margin of your screen with a [HRt] after each name:

    Susan
    Anthony
    Tami
    Ashley
    Noal
    Kym
    Shawn

2. *Block* (**Alt-F4** or **F12**) the list of names
3. Press *Sort* (**Ctrl-F9**)
4. Select **T**ype (7)
5. Select **L**ine (2)
6. Select **K**eys (3)
7. Set key1 so it looks like this:

Key	Typ	Field	Word
1	a	1	1

8. Press *Exit* (**F7**)
9. Press **P**erform Action (1)
10. Press *Exit* (**F7**) and select **N**o twice to clear the document window

Reminder:
If you have a name with a title such as Timothy J. Smith, Jr., keep the computer from sorting by the Jr., by using a hard space [ ] between the title and the last name. A hard space is inserted by pressing **Home** and **Spacebar**.

Lesson 4 Summary

WordPerfect has provided a great way to organize an outline for a database that can be used for merge purposes with primary documents.

The Sort feature may be used on an entire database to organize the information alphabetically or in any way desired.

The versatility continues as information may be blocked in a document and the block of data sorted.

Notes

Notes

LESSON

5

Select and Sort

The versatility of the WordPerfect Sort feature continues with the capability it offers to organize information from your database with the Select feature. The data can be accessed to choose specific lines, paragraphs, merges, or tables you want to work with. You can also use the "global" select capability for particular information from records.

This lesson will give you the basic steps for using the Select function and some examples for using Select and Sort together.

Basic Steps

The Select option enables you to pull information from your file. The select operation is performed by WordPerfect before the sorting procedure. The Sort feature, combined with the Select feature, enables you to pull out "like" information and organize reports or tables. For example, you may want to pull out like zip codes from an address database or the names of employees who work for a particular company. The basic steps for Select and Sort are as follows. The basics for sorting are reviewed before the Select operators are introduced.

- Press *Sort* (**Ctrl-F9**)

  The Sort menu offers you the following options:

  1 Merge, **2 S**ort, **3 C**onvert old Merge Codes.

- Choose *Sort* (2)

  The following message will appear in the lower left corner of the screen:

  Input file to sort: (Screen)

  You will be asked if you want the existing file on your screen to be sorted, or if you want to bring a file in at this point by pressing *Retrieve* (**Shift-F10**) and naming the file you want to sort.

- Press **Enter**

  The following prompt will appear in the lower left corner of the screen:

  Output file for sort: (Screen)

  You may choose to have the results of the sort appear on the screen or be stored in a new file on disk with a new file name.

NOTE

NOTE: If you choose to have the information go to a disk, you will want to avoid information loss in an existing file. Give the output from the sort a new file name so that the sorted information will be sent automatically to a file created on the disk.

- Press **Enter**

  The Sort screen will appear with the document in the top half of the screen and the Sort menu in the bottom half of the screen. Figure 5-1 shows you how a document and the Sort menu share the screen.

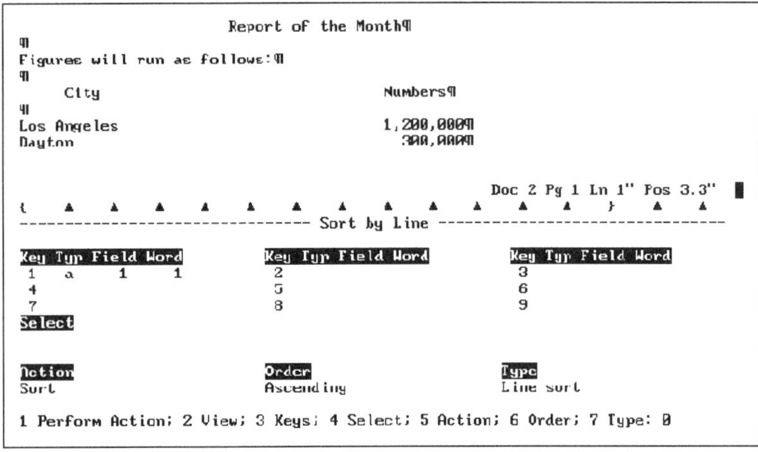

Figure 5-1

The parts of the *Sort* menu include:

Heading - the type of sort is indicated

Key fields - information is selected by priority order and placed in keys (1 through 9) according to the way you want the information sorted

Information area - describes actions such as sort, or sort and select, the order of the sort (ascending/descending), and the type of sort

Action items - the available sort options, which include Perform Action, View, Keys, Select, Action, Order, and Type

- Press **K**eys (3)

  The Key fields are where you choose the criteria by which your information will be sorted.

  a alphanumeric includes both letters and numbers of equal lengths.

  n numeric is used when you have numbers of unequal lengths.

  Sort keys should be defined before you run the Select function so WordPerfect will know which fields, lines, and words to use along with the select symbols. It is from the Sort menu that you create a select statement.

- Press *Exit* (**F7**)

  You will return to the Sort menu.

NOTE: Remember to save your document at this point before doing a select, as only the selected items will be in your output file.

- Decide on the Order (6) for the sort

  You can sort by ascending or descending order, alphabetically or numerically.

- Choose Select (**4**)

  You will create select statements that include defined keys and select symbols.

- Press Perform Action (**1**)

  Once all the criteria are in place, the sort may be performed.

NOTE: While WordPerfect is sorting, a counter at the bottom of the screen gives the count of the records being sorted.

Select

The Select feature in Sort will let you do exactly that—select information. The data can be numbers, groups of zip codes, dates; anything you want to select from your database. You select your data by creating a select statement during your sort that includes specified keys and select symbols.

The Select Symbols

The select symbols are defined as follows:

=

Records that have exactly the same information as indicated in a key would be selected.
Example: key3=801
Records would be selected containing the area code 801 only.

+ (OR)

Records would be selected if either statement in the record is true.
Example: key1=Jennifer + key2=East High School
Records would be searched to pull out Jennifer for key1 or East High School for key2.

* (AND)

Records that meet the conditions of both keys would be selected.
Example: key1=Jennifer * key2=East High School
Records would be selected to reflect all students by the name of Jeniffer attending East High School.

<>

Records that do not match information given in the identified key would be selected.
Example: key4<>Virginia
Records *not* containing the name Virginia in key4 would be selected.

>
Records that contain information greater than the information in the identified key would be selected.
Example: key2>90602
Records containing numbers greater than 90602 in key2 would be selected.

<
Records that contain information that is less than the information in the given key would be selected.
Example: key3<100,000
Records containing numbers less than 100,000 in key3 would be selected.

>=
Records that contain information greater than or equal to the information indicated in the key would be selected.
Example: key4>=100,000
Records containing numbers greater than or equal to 100,000 in key4 would be selected.

<=
Records that contain information less than or equal to the identified key would be selected.
Example: key3<=100,000
Records containing numbers less than or equal to 100,000 in key3 would be selected.

Other Select Conditions

A *global* select can be done to request all records that contain key words.
Example: keyg=Smith
All the records that have the name of Smith in any field would be selected.

The order of the select statement is left to right unless parentheses are used to change the order.

Example: key1=female * (key1=Smith + key2=Brown)

WordPerfect would look for all the names of Smith and Brown that are females.

Records may be selected *without* sorting them by the following steps:

- Select Action (5) from the Sort menu
- Choose Select Only (2)
- Create a select statement

Exercise 5.1 Selecting from Tabular Information

Try this exercise to see how the Select feature works.

1. Type the following information in tabular form with default margins of 1 inch and relative tabs set at 2.5 and 5 inches.

Dana L. Peterson	**Computer Technician**	**UT**
Cindy Herron	**Adolescent Educator**	**TN**
Sherri Simons	**Infant Specialist**	**VA**
Diane Birk	**Management Specialist**	**AZ**
Nicki Chidester	**Sports Therapist**	**UT**
Jonathan O. Jones	**Pediatric Care**	**NC**
Eleanore Erskine	**Geriatric Volunteer**	**NY**

2. Press *Save* (**F10**) to save the file as **SELECT1**

   You are now ready to enter the select statement. The first part of the instructions are to bring up the Sort menu.

3. Press *Sort* (**Ctrl-F9**)
4. Select Sort (2)

5. Press **Enter** twice

   You will sort the document on the screen and the output will also go to the screen.

   The default Sort screen, Sort by Line, appears as shown in Figure 5-2. If a different Sort screen heading appears, use the Type (7) option to change to Sort by Line.

Figure 5-2

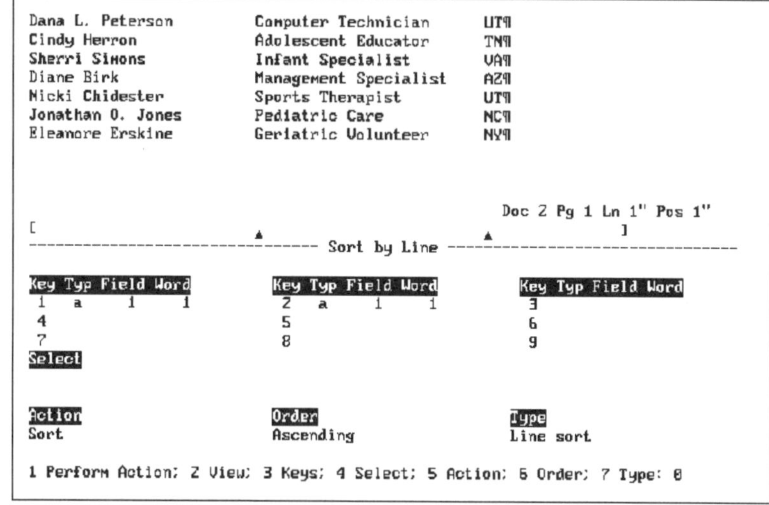

6. Select Keys (3)

   Information to be obtained from the records will be selected by select operators and the area the information is to be taken from will be identified in the keys. You will select the data records by entering the information in the field and word areas in key1 where the selected information may be found.

7. Set key1 as shown here:

Key	Typ	Field	Word
1	a	3	1

8. Press *Exit* (**F7**) and return to the Sort menu

9. Choose Select (4) to enter the select statement

   With the definition in key1, you are ready to give the system a select statement, which will include the key number and a comparison operator. In this example, key1 is equal to any records containing UT.

10. Type **Key1=UT**
11. Press *Exit* (**F7**)

    The cursor returns to the Sort menu.

12. Select Action (5)
13. Choose Select Only (2)

    Records from UT will be selected at this time, but not sorted alphabetically.

14. Press Perform Action (1)

    The result will be two records from UT.

Dana L. Peterson	Computer Technician	UT
Nicki Chidester	Sports Therapist	UT

15. Press *Exit* (**F7**) and select No twice to clear the document window

Using Sort and Select Together

The Sort feature may also be used when selecting information. The same basic steps are followed for setting up the sorting keys. Then the select statement is entered in the Select area and the sort is performed.

Exercise 5.2 Select and Sort

In this exercise, you will use the same sort priorities to select and sort the information in alphabetical order.

1. Press *Retrieve* (**Shift-F10**) and retrieve the file SELECT1

   The file contains the following list.

Dana L. Peterson	Computer Technician	UT
Cindy Herron	Adolescent Educator	TN
Sherri Simons	Infant Specialist	VA
Diane Birk	Management Specialist	AZ
Nicki Chidester	Sports Therapist	UT
Jonathan O. Jones	Pediatric Care	NC
Eleanore Erskine	Geriatric Volunteer	NY

2. Press *Sort* (**Ctrl-F9**)
3. Select Sort (2)
4. Press **Enter** twice to sort the document on the screen and to direct the output from the sort to the screen.

   The Sort by Line menu appears in the lower half of your screen.

   Information to be obtained from the records will be selected by select operators and the area the information is to be taken from will be identified in the keys.

5. Select Action (5)
6. Choose Select and Sort (1)
7. Press Perform Action (1)

   The information selected will be the two records from UT.

Nicki Chidester	Sports Therapist	UT
Dana L. Peterson	Computer Technician	UT

8. Press *Exit* (**F7**) and select No twice to clear the document window

Lesson 5 Summary

The Select function can gather specific information. The areas of information must be identified in the priority key area as to location of lines, fields, cells, and words.

Defining the priority key areas is the first step in the selection process. Select statements include the information from the key areas along with symbols.

The symbols include +, *, =, <>, >, <, >=, and <=.

A global select is indicated in the select area of the screen by typing **G** after key in the select area.

The Select function may be used alone to select specific information or with the Sort function to arrange the information.

Notes

Notes

Notes

LESSON

6

Additional Exercises

The way to review and reinforce what you have learned is to apply your newfound knowledge.

The exercises in this lesson cover line sort, paragraph sort, secondary merge sort, block sort, and select and sort.

Space is provided for you to make notes as you go through the exercises. Mark down anything you do not understand and need to review.

Line Sort

Exercise

1. Type the following tabular columns:

Tami Jensen	**Bell Elementary**
Corine Hall	**Two Peaks Elementary**
Gail Smith	**Brook Elementary**
Connie James	**Hansen Elementary**
Sherri Bell	**Brook Elementary**
Nancy Smith	**Two Peaks Elementary**

2. Press *Sort* (**Ctrl-F9**)
3. Select Sort (2)
4. Press **Enter** twice to bring the Sort menu to the screen
5. Select Keys (3) to define the following priorities:

Key1:	Type a, Field 1, Word -1
Key2:	Type a, Field 1, Word 1
Key3:	Type a, Field 2, Word 1

6. Press *Exit* (**F7**) to return to the Sort menu
7. Choose Select (4) and delete any select statement, if necessary; then press *Exit* (**F7**)
8. Select Perform Action (1)
9. Press *Save* (**F10**) and save the file as **ELTEACH**
10. Press *Exit* (**F7**) and select No twice to clear the document window

Notes

Secondary Merge Sort

Exercise

1. Type the following database information:

   Ms. Susan Smith{END FIELD}
   Vice President{END FIELD}
   Sampson Textiles{END FIELD}
   95 Apple Way
   Walnut Creek, CA 91254{END FIELD}
   {END RECORD}

   Mr. Dan Jaimez{END FIELD}
   Sales Manager{END FIELD}
   Holly Cars{END FIELD}
   1000 Madison Lane
   Salt Lake City, UT 84118{END FIELD}
   {END RECORD}

   Ms. Heather Smith{END FIELD}
   President{END FIELD}
   O.K. Insurance{END FIELD}
   346 Ohio Street
   Sacramento, CA 92365{END FIELD}
   {END RECORD}

2. Press *Save* (**F10**) and save the file as **DATA1**
3. Press *Sort* (**Ctrl-F9**)
4. Select Sort (2)
5. Press **Enter** twice
6. Select Type (7)

7. Choose **M**erge (1)
8. Select **K**eys (3)
9. Define the keys as follows:

   Key1: (last name)   Type a, Field 1, Line 1, Word -1
   Key2: (state)   Type a, Field 5, Line 1, Word -2

10. Press *Exit* (F7) to return to the Sort menu
11. Select **P**erform Action (1)
12. *Save* (**F10**) and name the file
13. Clear the document window

Notes

Paragraph Sort

Exercise

1. Retrieve the database file, DATA1, you typed in the preceding Secondary Merge exercise

   It should look like the following records.

   Ms. Susan Smith{END FIELD}
   Vice President{END FIELD}
   Sampson Textiles{END FIELD}
   95 Apple Way
   Walnut Creek, CA 91254{END FIELD}
   {END RECORD}

   Mr. Dan Jaimez{END FIELD}
   Sales Manager{END FIELD}
   Holly Cars{END FIELD}
   1000 Madison Lane
   Salt Lake City, UT 84118{END FIELD}
   {END RECORD}

   Ms. Heather Smith{END FIELD}
   President{END FIELD}
   O.K. Insurance{END FIELD}
   346 Ohio Street
   Sacramento, CA 92365{END FIELD}
   {END RECORD}

2. *Search* (**Alt-F2**) to locate and delete the {END FIELD} codes
3. *Search and Replace* (**Alt-F2**) {END RECORD} and any [HPg] codes with a [HRt] code
4. Press *Sort* (**CTRL-F9**) and choose Sort (2)
5. Choose Type (7) and select Paragraph (3)

6. Select **K**eys (3) and set the priorities as follows:

Key1: (last name)	Type a, Field 1, Line 1, Word -1
Key2: (city)	Type a, Field 5, Line 1, Word 1

7. Press *Exit* (**F7**)
8. Choose **P**erform Action (1)
9. Press *Save* (**F10**) to save and name the document
10. Press *Exit* (**F7**) and select **N**o twice to clear the document window

Notes

Block Sort

Exercise

1. Type the following list at the left margin:

    Sammy Holms
    Trina Valdez
    Margaret Hudson
    Anita Gomez
    John Holden

2. Move the cursor to the **S** in Sammy and *Block* (**Alt-F4** or **F12**) the list
3. Press *Sort* (**Ctrl-F9**) and choose Sort (2)
4. Select Type (7) and choose Line (2) sort, if necessary
5. Select Keys (3) and define the first priority key as follows:

    Key1: (last name)   Type a, Line 1, Word -1

6. Press *Exit* (**F7**) to return to the Sort menu
7. Select Perform Action (1)
8. *Save* (**F10**) your document
9. Clear the document window

Notes

Select and Sort

Exercise

1. Retrieve the secondary database file, DATA1, you typed in the Secondary Merge exercise

   Ms. Susan Smith{END FIELD}
   Vice President{END FIELD}
   Sampson Textiles{END FIELD}
   95 Apple Way
   Walnut Creek, CA 91254{END FIELD}
   {END RECORD}

   Mr. Dan Jaimez{END FIELD}
   Sales Manager{END FIELD}
   Holly Cars{END FIELD}
   1000 Madison Lane
   Salt Lake City, UT 84118{END FIELD}
   {END RECORD}

   Ms. Heather Smith{END FIELD}
   President{END FIELD}
   O.K. Insurance{END FIELD}
   346 Ohio Street
   Sacramento, CA 92365{END FIELD}
   {END RECORD}

2. Press *Sort* (**Ctrl-F9**) and choose **S**ort (2)
3. Select **M**erge (1) as the **T**ype (7) of sort
4. Define **K**eys (3) as follows:

Key1: (last name)	Type a, Field 1, Line 1, Word -1
Key2: (zip code)	Type a, Field 5, Line 1, Word -1

5. Press *Exit* (**F7**) to return to the Sort menu
6. Define **S**elect (4) as follows:

   Key2>90000 * Key2<91000

7. Choose **A**ction (1)
8. Choose **S**elect and Sort (1)
9. Choose **P**erform Action (1)
10. *Save* (**F10**) the document and clear the document window

Notes

Global Select

Exercise

When you perform a global select, you define the global search by typing a **G** after the word Key.

1. Type the table as follows (accept the default margins and set the relative tabs at 2 and 4 inches)

Lisa Henrie	**Sally's Salon**	**Murray, UT 84107**
Jefferey Day	**The Cut**	**San Francisco, CA 91032**
Damon Trust	**Great Looks**	**New York, NY 11078**
Devin Lloyd	**Looking Great**	**Brenton, OH 35621**
Ted Hansen	**Great Looks**	**Seattle, WA 74356**
Kyle Evan	**Almonds**	**Silver Spring, MD 13578**

2. Press *Save* (**F10**) and name the file
3. Press *Sort* (**Ctrl-F9**) and choose Sort (2)
4. Press **Enter** twice
5. Choose Type (7) then Line (2)
6. Choose Select (4)
7. Type: **KeyG=Great Looks**
8. Press **Enter**
9. Select Action (5)
10. Choose Select Only (2)
11. Select Perform Action (1)
12. *Save* (**F10**) the document and clear the document window

Notes

Sort and Select Terms

Action The Action option is used in connection with the Select feature. Action has two: Select, and Sort and Select Only. A select statement must be entered in the select area before this feature can be used.

Fields The field area depends on the type of sort you are doing; for example, line sort (lines and paragraph), merge sort (lines), or table sort (rows).

Keys The areas where sorting priorities are defined based on which lines, paragraphs, merge records, or rows are used for the sorting criteria. There are nine priority keys to sort by.

Line In the default setting of Line sort, lines are considered a record. Lines are generally counted from the top of the record, but can be counted from the bottom of the record by using a minus sign in front of the number.

Order The sort may be conducted in ascending order (A to Z with numbers going from 0 to 9) or in descending order (Z to A with letters and numbers sorted in reverse order).

Perform Action Begins the sorting or selecting.

Records The line sort will end with a [SRt] or a [HRt]. A paragraph sort must end with two [HRt]. In the merge sort, records are separated by {End Record}. The table sort uses rows as record designations.

Select Information may be extracted from files by using particular symbols to indicate like information and certain parameters of information. Selection is done based on the select statement, which reads from left to right.

Type The type option changes the type of sort being conducted. The options are: Line, Paragraph, and Merge. You can also sort information stored in a table.

Words Words can be separated by spaces, forward slashes (/), and by hard hyphens (**Home,-**) in a line or field. Words generally are counted from the left, but they may be counted from the right with a minus sign (-).

NOTES

NOTES